TEWKESBURY
& THE VALE OF GLOUCESTER
IN OLD PHOTOGRAPHS

How to make a thong to tie a sheaf. Mrs Watkins and her grand-daughter Emmie. 1905. Forthampton.

TEWKESBURY
& THE VALE OF GLOUCESTER
IN OLD PHOTOGRAPHS

COLLECTED BY

CHARLES HILTON

ALAN SUTTON
1987

Alan Sutton Publishing Limited
Brunswick Road · Gloucester

First published 1987

British Library Cataloguing in Publication Data

Tewkesbury in old photographs.
1. Tewkesbury (Gloucestershire) —
. History
I. Hilton, Charles
942.4'12   DA690.T36

ISBN 0-86299-416-0

Cover:
This dancing bear, owned by an itinerant showman, performed in Barton Street in 1900. It excited children, and besides farthings, halfpennies and pennies received by the showman, sweets, buns and stale bread were also donated.

Typesetting and origination by
Alan Sutton Publishing Limited.
Printed in Great Britain

CONTENTS

1905. The organ-grinder outside Southfield House, Forthampton. He would usually receive a penny or so for his efforts, and something to eat.

INTRODUCTION

The Vale of Gloucester, comprising some 50,000 acres, is tucked between the Vale of Berkeley to the south and the Vale of Evesham to the north. The ancient market town of Tewkesbury lies at its northern end, and from the promontory of the Mythe Tute just north of the town, the view takes in most of the western part of the Vale. From this same point, the eastern part, while somewhat obscured, generally appears flat until it abruptly comes to an end along the 1000 feet high escarpments of the Cotswold Edge.

The history of the Vale over the centuries has been much influenced by its topography, and particularly by the large river Severn which drains it. Salmon, eels, elvers, and lampreys have been fished for centuries, and in the Tewkesbury area coarse fishing was, and still is, a great attraction.

For centuries the river has also been important as a means of transporting goods. Until the coming of the railways during the nineteenth century, it was busy with barge and boat traffic. Prominently among them were the famous Severn trows, the biggest of which displaced over 80 tons. They sported a mast, 80 feet high, and carried a large area of sail. A miscellaneous collection of small craft carried cargoes of five or six tons, and their trade was particularly connected with the small villages situated near the banks of the river. In the eighteenth and early nineteenth centuries gangs of eight men, known as 'bow halliers', pulled barges along the river by means of a rope-harness. They were displaced by horses in 1830.

There were other barges or frigates which plied their trade. Some were 40 to 60 feet in length, with a single mast and square sail, carrying cargoes of 20 to 40 tons. In 1756 as many as four hundred of these vessels were working the Severn. The crews who navigated the trows often augmented their wind power by attaching a tow-boat to the bow of their craft and, with the aid of 18 foot-long oars, got up a good rate of knots. They also made use of the Severn bore, but occasionally got into severe difficulties when the trow overtook the tow boat.

Commodities which were transported along the Severn were coal, grain, flour, malt, wool, tallow, rope, shoes, drapery and dyed stuffs, barrels, gloves, mustard balls, nails, stockings, cotton-thread, lace, and a wide range of ironmongery.

The nineteenth century saw the introduction of steam barges and, for a time, these had both sail and steam. However, with the improvement in engines, trows and other craft which relied solely upon wind-power, were totally displaced. During the present century oil-tankers delivered oil to Severnside depots. Then, after the war, road tankers were found to be more convenient. Other than a small number of motorised grain-barges employed by Allied Mills (Healings), and some pleasure craft, the Severn in the Vale is less busy than in the past.

The Avon, which forms the county boundary for a short distance, joins the Severn at Tewkesbury. It, too, was used for the transport of goods, but the vessels concerned were on a smaller scale than those on the Severn. For boating and sailing for pleasure, however, especially in Victorian and Edwardian times, the Avon was more popular than the Severn, and even today it is crowded with boats of all descriptions. Its coarse fishing still provides fishermen, who come mainly from the Midlands, with plenty of sport.

In medieval times the natural course of the Avon was altered at Tewkesbury through the making of a more-or-less straight cut – the New Avon – with its outfall into the Severn at Lower Lode. Its purpose was to provide a sufficient fall of water to drive the waterwheels of the several mills erected along its course.

Both rivers have a natural flood-plain to the north-west of Tewkesbury. For the most part they now only cover the flat meadow land known as the Ham, but in the past, parts of the town were often flooded. For centuries the Ham has produced excellent grass, not only because of its rich alluvial soil, but because rich mineral deposits are left behind when the flood-waters subside. Hay is taken as a first crop to the benefit of the town's finances, and the aftermath is grazed by sheep and cattle to the benefit of those who still hold common rights. Flooding of the low-lying meadows in the Vale, if not too extreme, helps to produce rich pastures for dairy and beef cattle.

In the past, travellers on foot, on horseback, or by carriage, from the west, entered Tewkesbury by crossing the Severn by two ferries, situated respectively at the Lower Lode at Forthampton and the Upper Lode at the Mythe. In 1823 the owners of the latter ferry were bought out so that a bridge could be built in its place, and Thomas Telford undertook its construction. It was named Mythe Bridge, and opened for traffic in 1826. As for the Lower Lode ferry, it continued to function just into the 1970s, and was then closed.

A much older bridge is the one that spans the Avon at Tewkesbury. Because its total length was almost half a mile, it came to be known as the Long Bridge. King John ordered two spans to be built of stone and gave the tolls of the Wednesday and Saturday markets for its upkeep. The stone arches were extended in 1747 to four, and the wooden bridge was gradually replaced by a solid causeway. The present-day bridge was widened and rebuilt in stone and concrete in 1962.

Another Severn bridge of note is Haw Bridge, Tirley. For centuries the river was forded at this point, and was known as the Haw Passage. The bridge built in 1825 was damaged by a runaway barge in 1958, and the present bridge was opened three years later.

Tewkesbury, as a town, developed on the comparatively high ground between the New Avon and the smaller Swilgate river. The old street plan takes the form of a Y, and consists of High Street, Barton Street and Church Street. All converge near the site of the former market cross, at the war memorial.

Tewkesbury was not extremely affected by the impact of the Industrial Revolution during the nineteenth century, and so ended up by having many of its old and historic buildings intact. The street façades provide a wide range of architecture from timber-framed Tudor and Jacobean buildings, with over-hanging upper storeys and steep-pitched gables, to red brick Queen Anne, Georgian and Victorian specimens. Many have been converted into shops and offices which, inevitably, have led to modifications, but enough style has been preserved to make the town attractive.

In the past, the town had a substantial stage-coach trade. Several inns were established alongside the three main streets to cater for the needs of travellers, and to provide stabling for the horses. These still exist, but have been modernised to meet the needs of today. All, however, have managed to retain something of their historic charm and interest.

The building which, in itself, contains the greatest variety of architectural interest, is the great Abbey church sited to the south of the town. Most of it is Norman, with later additions. Its long history has been the subject of many books, for within it are the tombs of monarchs and the once powerful lords of Tewkesbury who successively influenced the fortunes of the nation over many centuries. It suffered desecration during the Lancastrian and Yorkist struggle at Bloody Meadow, only a stone's throw away, and had to adapt to the occupation by both Royalist and Parliamentary forces in the see-saw struggles during the Civil Wars of the seventeenth century.

The Vale of Gloucester is almost entirely agricultural, with unspoilt villages and few industries. Its varied soils have always produced rich grass on which beef and dairy cattle as well as sheep have been raised. The famous Gloucester cheeses were produced in quantity at the farmhouses. Hedges, hedgerow trees, farmsteads, and cottages encircled with orchard trees are characteristic of the area.

One sad feature is the closure of village schools and the transfer of the children to larger ones. Many churches, too, have been amalgamated, with one incumbent looking after the needs of several parishes.

Deerhurst is a parish with Saxon origins, with visible examples of the work of Saxon masons. A number of enormous tithe barns, such as that at Ashleworth, are of special interest. Many of the villages which lie close to the banks of the Severn still retain the old wharves from which coal and other commodities were unloaded when the river was their lifeline. Wheat, barley and oats were also despatched from these same wharves for grinding into flour and feeding-stuffs at the Tewkesbury mills.

To wander through the miles of narrow lanes within the Vale is to capture a little of the old world charm of a century ago.

Until the coming of the railways, the two rivers had been the commercial life-line for Tewkesbury. The tug shown here pulled barges laden with grain, flour, coal, coke and bricks, during the late thirties and into the forties.

King John's Bridge over the Avon, 1890. Originally, King John built two spans in stone, hence the name.

1906. The Avon above King John's Bridge; for centuries a popular area for boating and fishing.

1906. The Avon, showing where the old railway bridge spanned it. The bridge was pulled down in the 1960s under the Beeching 'axe'.

11

Bathurst's Yard, 1909, was busy with boat-building and hiring out all kinds of pleasure craft.

1905. The transfer of boats from the Avon to the Severn, and vice versa, was made through the lock in front of the lock-keeper's lodge on the left.

The New Avon and old sluice gates, 1900.

23410A. TEWKESBURY. KING JOHN'S BRIDGE. — JUDGES 119.

The medieval and Tudor buildings on either side of the newer lamp-standard housed the brewery and wine store of Bayliss and Merrel.

1900. The Borough Flour Mills (Healings) lie ahead with old industries along the left bank.

1890. The tall-masted Severn trows carried grain and flour to and from the mills in competition with steam-driven barges.

Barges and trows at Tewkesbury quay in the eighteenth century.

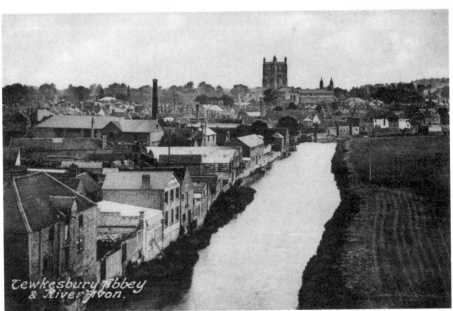

1900. The Ham is on the right, and its grass has been cut for hay. The old industrial warehouses are on the left.

1904. Trips to Upton-on-Severn were popular at this time. Passengers are here seen boarding the pleasure-cruiser from King John's Island (south).

Tewkesbury from the Severn Meadows.

During the nineteenth century the gangs of eight men who pulled the barges were displaced by horses. 1903.

1900. Practising for the Tewkesbury Regatta, held annually but now discontinued.

Twyning Sleet, on the Avon.

Published by W. L. Foxon, Castle Street, Hinckley.

Popular excursions from Tewkesbury were also those to Twyning, about two miles up the Avon. They ended, at the point where the ferry was situated, seen here in 1902. The inn, on the right, provided food and drink.

Part of Twyning village, 1900.

Tewkesbury Regatta in 1908, as seen from the Ham. Some rowing eights started at Twyning Fleet and ended at Tewkesbury.

Twyning is a spacious village, with two greens. The cart is carrying a governess and her charge. 1903.

1890. This timber-framed house, with its massive chimney, is typical of several others in the village.

Binders, such as the one at work here in Twyning, were a common sight on farms from the 1920s to the 1950s when they were gradually superseded by combine-harvesters.

Binders automatically tied the corn into sheaves which were then hand-stacked into shocks or stooks to dry.

Potato pickers ready for work during the Second World War. Schools had a week's holiday in October so that children could give a hand.

The Jubilee was one of three pleasure steamers owned by Bathurst. The Edwardian ladies and gentlemen have been on an outing to Upton-on-Severn.

The Severn at the Mythe is now used less for boating and sailing than it was when this photograph was taken at the turn of the century.

Mythe Bridge, looking north, was built by Thomas Telford, and opened in 1826. The old water-tower, since demolished, was built in 1889.

1936. This ancient look-out hill was possibly raised by the Saxons so that warning could be had of invading Danes. It gave a clear view both of the Severn and the Vale of Gloucester. Mrs Selina Strickland sold the Mythe Tute, on which it was built, to the Borough of Tewkesbury, for £14 14s. 0d. Woad grows on the red-marl cliffs facing the river on its far side.

King John's Castle in 1904. The tower is the only part left of the original extensive buildings demolished in 1539.

1904. The Severn, looking north from the Mythe Tute. The pools on the right are old clay pits from which clay was dug for brickmaking during the last century.

1930. This water tower at the top of Mythe Hill was built in 1889, and its water supply was piped to Cheltenham for street cleaning ten years later. It became redundant after the extension of Mythe Water Works in 1921. It has only recently been converted into a dwelling.

Paget's Lane was part of the Ancient Salt Way which led to Droitwich. The bridge, photographed in 1904, was demolished in the 1920s. It linked the Mythe Tute with the grounds of King John's Castle. George III walked over it on the occasion of his visits to the Tute in July 1788. Thereafter the Tute was referred to on Ordnance Survey maps as Royal Hill.

A lock and weir were built at the Upper Lode, Tewkesbury, to aid navigation on the Severn. They were opened in 1858. The lady in the crinoline was the first lock-keeper's wife.

This is the same house c. 1930. A few changes are obvious.

A general view of the lock, c. 1930. The lamp to the right was similar to a domestic oil-lamp, and needed priming every day.

The S.S. *Atalanta* is in the lock awaiting its filling.

The Old Severn after the lock had been cut. Much of it has silted up. Ferry farm (left), had been a licensed house since 1565. The haystack is raised on staddle stones against the frequent floods.

1950. The lock underwent a thorough cleaning and repair. In 1986 it was again emptied and repaired.

Tewkesbury's old tanneries by the Avon. It is from these that Mrs Craik had the idea for her novel, *John Halifax, Gentleman*. Milner & Co., took over the premises in 1908 as an ironmongery store.

1900. The cottages on the left are a mixture of medieval and Tudor design, with later alterations. The pump, with its stone trough, supplied drinking water for all who lived close by.

Bell Hotel, Tewkesbury, Home of Abel Fletcher (John Halifax, Gentleman)

1912. Originally the guest house of the abbot in medieval times, the hotel advertises Arnold Perret's ales and offers stabling for horses.

The roof fire occurred in 1921. Note the motor bike and side-car with its churn of water and the onlooker in widow's weeds.

The house on the extreme edge of the photograph was part of the town's grammar school in 1900. In 1904 a new school was built in the gardens adjoining, and is now the town library. In 1970 the house shown here was pulled down to make the Bell Hotel car park. The hotel had a famous bowls green of ancient origin, but this has recently been built over.

1904. Another association with Mrs Craik's novel in which John Halifax featured as a self-taught man. This was his study.

The miller is viewing his cargo of wheat brought from farms within the Vale of Gloucester. 1904.

1907. This view, from the Ham, gives the SW side of the mill, and shows the buttressed outer wall of the old monastic barn, with the abbey in the background.

Victoria Jubilee Gardens were opened on 22 June 1897 on land between the New Avon and the Gloucester Road. The cannon was captured from the Russians during the Crimean War of 1854–1856.

A quiet Sunday afternoon at Abbey Mill. The mill dates from 1793, but the abbey monks worked a mill here in 1190.

The Abbey Mill, Tewkesbury.

1909. The mill had four large water-wheels driving eight pairs of millstones in 1793. Here, it has three wheels remaining. Mill Street cottages are to the right.

St Mary's Lane, and entrance to the former tan-yards, 1904. Streets now had some gas-lighting. Stocking weavers' cottages begin at the right side of the photograph.

Tewkesbury Abbey.

1906. The abbey as seen from the Bell Hotel. The gates were erected by Lord Gage in 1734, and designed by William Edney, a Bristol smith.

1904. The nave, looking east. The piers are 6ft. 3 ins. in diameter and 30ft. 8ins. high.

Tewkesbury Abbey and vicarage at the turn of the century. (South view).

1904. West end of the Abbey with its massive window. The join of the original roof can be seen on the tower. The present vaulted roof was built in the mid fourteenth century.

1900. The dominance of the Abbey tower is here seen to advantage. The family cricket match taking place was made possible because the Borough Council persuaded the owner of the Ham to set aside a small area of meadow for recreation purposes. Access to the Ham was, and still is, by a footbridge beside the mill.

1904. The Abbey and the River Swilgate in a rural setting to the south.

The Swilgate is liable to flooding during heavy rainfall, as here in 1905. In 1770 its waters flooded the Abbey floors to a depth of several inches.

1904. The buttresses of the medieval monastery barn show up clearly here. The roof was incorporated in Victorian times and the building was later used as the Fitzhamon Art Gallery.

This 1908 picture shows the tall elm trees which typified the area until they were wiped out by Dutch Elm disease in the 1970s. There is no firm evidence that Queen Margaret, who led the Lancastrian forces in the Battle of Tewkesbury in 1471, ever set up camp here.

The Abbot's Gatehouse, early Tudor, and faced with yellow limestone from Guiting in the Cotswolds.

1904. Detail of the Abbey tower showing the three stages of its construction by the Normans.

The Abbey Choir (east), 1904.

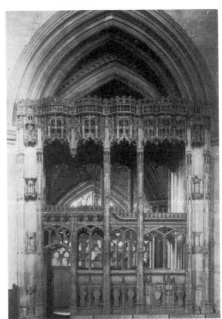

The Warwick chapel, erected in 1430 by Isabel Despenser in memory of her first husband, Richard Beauchamp. 1904.

The Choir Ambulatory, fourteenth century. 1904.

The so-called Wakeman Cenotaph, with a snake, frog, mouse, and snail eating the corpse.

The Chantry Tomb of Sir Edward Spenser, Lord of Tewkesbury from 1359 to 1375.

1890. Mrs Craik's (Dinah Maria Mulock) memorial in the Abbey. Her novel, *John Halifax, Gentleman*, was published in 1857, and became a best seller. It has recently been reprinted as a paperback.

The Grove mausoleum in Tewkesbury cemetery. It was built in 1897 with four feet of concrete as a foundation, with heavy, buttressed walls and an extra strong roof of thick tiles, enough to withstand an earthquake. The Revd C. Grove gave the Grove organ to Tewkesbury Abbey in 1887 among many other gifts.

Merry-go-round in Barton Street, 1914. It was a product of Walker and Sons at the Oldbury, Tewkesbury. The firm had a big export trade in this kind of equipment.

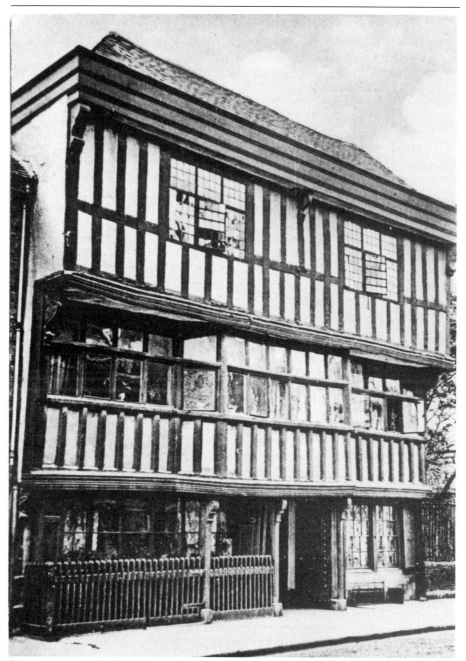

Originally the home of a succession of prosperous merchants from early Tudor times, it is now the town museum, Barton Street, and has changed but little since the photograph was taken in 1904.

1908. J.W. Tysoe's cheese warehouse in Barton Street. Double Gloucester cheese, a product of the Vale of Gloucester, was among the many cheeses to be had.

The Ashchurch road proceeds from Barton Street, and Walton Spa pump-room was built in 1835. It was never used as such, and was demolished in 1961.

1860. Interior of the Patent Renewable Stocking Factory. Stocking knitting had for long been a cottage industry in Tewkesbury, but has now become industrialised under the factory system.

High Street before 1900. It is still the age of the horse.

1898. The men with the dog are drovers. They brought in cattle and sheep from farms far and wide in the Vale.

In 1890 Tewkesbury's fat and store cattle market was held fortnightly on alternate Wednesdays by Mr George Hone and Messrs. Moore and Sons. Mr Hone also had a saleyard near Trinity Church. This scene, May 1927, is of Mr L. Hone selling sheep in his new market on the old site near Trinity Church.

Horseback riding into town, on market days especially, was a feature of life in the High Street in 1890. The street, still partly cobbled, was lit by gas supplied by the Tewkesbury Gas Works established in 1833. The bicycle on the right was a popular model at this time.

1900. The Coffee House on the left of High Street was the favourite meeting place for farmers' wives on market days. It also advertised 'well-aired beds, fresh cakes daily, and good accommodation for tourists, with home comforts.'

1900. Hayward and Sons was founded in 1820. It is now the oldest family business in town, still in the High Street.

High Street 1891. The clock over the old post office was presented to the town in 1883 by Alderman C. Smart, mayor.

High Street, 1900, with its façade of shops. Papps was the largest drapery store in the district.

High Street, 1890. The Swan Hotel was once a busy coaching inn. The one-horse carriage took guests to and from the railway station.

1890. The balcony over the old coach entrance was used to announce the results of national and local elections, and for MPs to make speeches.

The old Coach House, Tewkesbury. Mallett, Photo, Tewkesbury.

The Nodding Gables gained its name from a break in the attic ridge. It was once the ticket office and depot for stage coaches. It dates from the fifteenth century, but was altered in Tudor times.

THE ANCIENT COURT HOUSE, TEWKESBURY. 77816. J.V.

The High Street has many notable buildings, as the next dozen pictures of 1904 will show. Cross or Court House is mainly fifteenth and sixteenth century, and is said to have been the Court House of the Lords of Tewkesbury.

The signs indicate the purpose of this sixteenth-century building. It was well-used for public functions. According to Gardner's Visitors Guide of 1890, the Old Theatre entrance was at the Wheatsheaf.

Clarence House also dates from the fifteenth century, with later alterations. It is said that the Duke of Clarence occasionally dwelt here – the same Clarence supposedly drowned in a butt of Malmsey wine. His vault is in the Abbey.

The hospital functioned as such from 1865 to 1934. It then became the Borough Council Offices. Situated at the Oldbury, it is easily accessible from High Street.

This interior of the Tudor, timber-framed Ancient Grudge, shows the fine moulded timber beams.

1890, looking towards the Cross. It shows the Nodding Gables, Clarence House opposite and Cross House adjoining the clock.

The Town Hall was built in 1788 as a gift to the corporation by Sir William Codrington. It had an open forecourt, intended as a Corn Market, but in 1857 it was enclosed by a stone building in the classical tradition, as seen here.

The façade is dated here as 1897, but its main structure is seventeenth-century. It was a Nonconformist academy from 1712 to 1719.

Eventually the Old Academy became the Tudor House Hotel. John Moore, the Tewkesbury author, spent some of his childhood here when it was a dwelling house.

The panelled Mayor's Parlour, seventeenth-century, is still one of the delights of the Tudor House Hotel.

Tewkesbury, One of the Ancient Timbered Houses.

1908. The Black Bear Inn, reputed to be the oldest inn in Gloucestershire. It was founded in 1308. The wooden stocks of the town stood under the elm tree.

The High Street frontage, looking north, in 1890. The blacksmith's shop is on the right. The inn was used by farmers as an unofficial corn-exchange.

Mitton Manor House was used during the 1914–1918 war as a hospital for wounded servicemen.

1920. Church Street, showing the transition between the horse and the motor car age.

This Edwardian scene shows the rear of Barsanti's restaurant in Church Street. He stocked it with statues to remind him of his beloved Italy.

Church Street from the Cross, 1900. Ye Olde Berkeley Arms advertised 'Accommodation for Cyclists', a recreational pastime for leisured men and women which was all the rage.

1924. A garage workshop in St Mary's Lane, tooled to meet the needs of the new motor-age.

1908. Mallet's news agency and Mrs Brick's confection and tobacco shop on the left.

1908. Church Street with the Old Hat Shop opposite the man on his bicycle. The old post-office is by the lamp-standard.

The bull-nosed Morris car opposite the Hop Pole Hotel, and beside Warwick House, gives the date at about 1926. The timber-framed house on the extreme left used to be called the Old Curiosity Shop. J.M. Turner, the artist, stayed there for some time. The timber-framed Warwick House was gutted by fire a few years ago, but is soon due to be restored.

Church Street from the War Memorial Cross, built on the site of the former ancient Market Cross in 1920.

The dresses of the people in this Church Street scene are typical of the late Victorian and early Edwardian eras.

Church Street in the 1920s. Not a horse in sight! The timber-framed Berkeley Arms is fifteenth century with later additions.

The Royal Hop Pole Hotel was a former coaching inn, made famous by Dickens in his Pickwick papers.

1903. Tewkesbury High School, Church Street. Senior pupils were prepared for examination by Universities, the Board of Education, the Royal Academy, the Royal College of Music and the Royal Drawing Society.

Old Baptist Chapel, Church Street, dates from 1623, and this 1920 photograph shows it before its restoration in 1977.

The former Richardson's Almshouses in the 1930s. They were pulled down in 1966 to make way for up-to-date buildings.

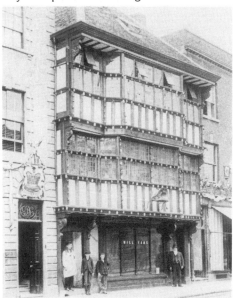

The Old Hat Shop, Church Street, with its Beadle-hat sign.

1911. Lilley's Alley, Church Street, and one of Tewkesbury's most attractive features. A malthouse and clay-pipe manufactory were sited here.

At the turn of the century; the Fair is coming to town.

This scene is of the very high flood of 1947. Church Street was flooded, and its continuation into the Gloucester Road, as seen here, shows the extent.

An Edwardian summer's day beside the Mill Avon.

Lower Lode Lane, leading from Tewkesbury to Forthampton, across the Severn. 1900.

The Lower Lode Ferry, Tewkesbury side. It carried pedestrians and vehicles to Forthampton, and gave access to other villages in the Vale of Gloucester.

The same ferry, in 1890, with horses and vehicles waiting for its return from the Forthampton side.

Ferry and Lower Lode Hotel, Forthampton. 1905. For centuries the ferry was the only means of crossing into Tewkesbury from the west and north.

Circa 1908. An outing to the Lower Lode Hotel. The guests came by one of the pleasure cruisers which plied the Severn.

Forthampton Church and old workhouse established in 1793, seen here in 1870. The workhouse took in 'aged and infirm paupers, orphan children, idlers, and others' who were a burden on the community.

Forthampton Court and garden, 1870. Mrs P. Yorke and Mrs C.A. Cooke are viewing the park.

1870. Walking the plank! The ha-ha kept parkland cattle and sheep from the house and gardens.

Forthampton Court sitting-room in 1903, showing roof beams of the former medieval hall. The room was restored to its original dimensions in 1914.

1865. Mr Joseph Yorke, squire of the Forthampton estate, talking with his bailiff Mr Lockart (on horseback), but Clyde, the dog, shows little interest.

1870. Mrs J.R. Yorke, Mme de Brienen, and Mrs Langhorne at archery on Forthampton Court lawn.

1865. Augustus Yorke (3 years) with governess and pet donkey.

1870. The estate gamekeeper with a plentiful bag of rabbits.

Fashion, 1895! Forthampton estate-workers' wives and friends.

Corner House Farm and barns, Forthampton. The heap of stones will be broken up and used to mend the pot-holes in the road, 1905.

1905. Emanuel Cole breaking the heap of stones. He was also responsible for trimming the road verges by hand.

1870. Gardening staff in Forthampton Court gardens with horse-drawn mower-roller.

Leah Newbury washing clothes at her tub. In 1905 households were run on a strict routine of activities for each day of the week, except on a Sunday, the day of rest.

The harvest at Forthampton in 1905 being scythed by Charles Roan and others.

The Secret! Harry Turberville and his sister. At the turn of the century slates were in daily use in schools, especially for arithmetic.

Forthampton Court 1870. A quiet game of cards.

Bishop's Walk, 1910, was possibly so-called because of Forthampton's connection with Tewkesbury monastery. The Bishop of Worcester was Lord of the Manor in 1751.

1910. The Old Forge at Forthampton. Corner House Farm is on the right. Prior to the Second World War, village blacksmiths not only shod horses, but repaired almost every kind of farm implement.

Forthampton 1870. This well is in the grounds of Church View, formerly the Almshouses. It is also known as 'the whistling well' because, it is said, the Severn Bore forces air through cracks in the rocks leading to the well.

Estate cottages built in the nineteenth century. Their high quality indicates that they were architecturally designed.

Meet of the Ledbury Hounds at Forthampton Cottage, February 19th, 1909.

Hunting has changed but little since 1909. The giant elm trees, however, have succumbed to disease during the last decade.

1940. One of the early combine harvesters at work at Corner House Farm, Forthampton. The newer models of today have reduced the labour force required to run them.

Bagging and weighing the corn taken from the combine harvester.

Forthampton cricket team, 1914. W. Dutton, W. Crockett, F. Smith, T. Davies (b.r) W. Finch, F. Wilkins, B. Newbury, Revd Wall, F. Fowler (m.r), B. Davies and B. Spry.

1920. RAOB charabanc outing from Tewkesbury to the Wye valley. Increasingly, cricket and football teams used such transport for away matches.

1910. The blacksmith's and post office are on the right. The raised footpath aided pedestrians in flood-times. On the left is the one-time village shop.

St Mary's church is an Anglo-Saxon building of the first order. Some of it was there in 804, with restoration in the tenth century. The exterior walls show areas of herring-bone work. The photograph was taken in 1904.

1901. The two-light window with pointed heads is pure Saxon, as is the blocked doorway. The triangular eyes are also Saxon and may represent 'the eyes of God.'

1901. The beautiful late ninth-century font.

1901. Odda's Chapel, Deerhurst. It was built in 1056, and restored in 1885. The timber-framed farmhouse adjoining it is of the sixteenth century.

Rose Cottage, old almshouses and other property. 1949.

A different view of the old almshouses. They were derelict in 1958, and shortly afterwards were pulled down.

Happy group of Deerhurst children with their headmaster, Mr W. Fluck and staff. 1940s.

The BBC produced radio programmes during the 1940s for primary schools, in which games and informal PE featured prominently, with a background of music.

Reminiscent of the war years and some years afterwards. The midday hot meal arrives at a time of high floods at Deerhurst village school.

Deerhurst flood, 1947. Unwillingly to school? Not in this case!

Children with their teachers observe the midget submarine, known as the 'Shrimp', which was making a trip up-Severn to Tewkesbury. This craft was developed during the last war to torpedo enemy craft in harbours.

Deerhurst's school milk being dispensed straight from the milkman's can. School milk was supplied for children during the last war, a service which has since been retained for primary schools.

During the war years oil tankers were active along the Severn, but their wash caused erosion problems along many parts of the banks, particularly where bends in the river occurred.

Further down the Severn from Deerhurst and Apperley is Wainlode Hill which borders the Severn as high, red-marl cliffs. 1903.

The Headmaster of Deerhurst school, Mr W. Fluck, with his pupils, surveying a bank to determine the yearly speed of erosion. The two trees on the right toppled into the water soon after this 1945 photograph was taken.

Some of Deerhurst's roads were subject to deep flooding, and wooden boards or 'stanks' were slotted into the posts permanently fixed in the roadside banks to hold the waters at bay. Clay was used to seal any gaps or cracks among the boards. This 1941 scene is along the Deerhurst–Apperley road.

In this case the 'stanks' were erected and sealed in good time, and the flood waters are effectively held back.

1950. Len Roberts cutting withies for basket-making at Severnside, Deerhurst. The osier beds were properly managed so that each year a suitable supply was assured.

Withy beds on the right, and the stacked end-product ready to be carted away.

1945. A milking herd of dairy shorthorns, a popular breed of cattle which has since been superseded by the black and white Friesian breed. The donkey attached to the herd at all times was, so it was believed, a safeguard against the herd being affected by contagious abortion. This myth was common in other parts of the country as well as at Deerhurst.

Preparing salmon nets on the banks of the Severn at Deerhurst some thirty years ago.

The salmon net in position and ready to be hauled in.

Apperley Cricket Club, 1906. Top row left to right: W. Margrett, C. Smith, A.E. Margrett, A.E. Dipper (a Gloucestershire and England player), W. Green, A. George, C. Crook, F. Tribble. Front row seated: A. Dipper (father), A. Roberts, S.J. Gillet (Mayor of Gloucester), A. Glover, A. Smith, and W. Mann. The boy is Mr Gillet's son.

Ashleworth, a few miles down the Severn from Deerhurst and Apperley, has a church dating from 1100, but is interesting because of its architectural features of later periods. 1904 photograph.

1904. This famous tithe barn was built between 1481–1515. It is 125ft. long, 25ft. wide, has ten bays and is under the aegis of the National Trust.

Typical willow country round Ashleworth.

The Old Vicarage, Ashleworth, Glos. Brooke Gloucester.

1890. Striking timber-framed house of the sixteenth century.

1890. Ashleworth Manor House, of fifteenth century origin.

1947. Ashleworth Manor House after structural alterations. This year saw high floods in villages bordering the Severn.

1870. S. and H. Fulljames outside the Old Vicarage, Ashleworth.

Severnside at Ashleworth, 1937.

Awaiting the ferry on the Sandhurst bank, Ashleworth, in the early 1940s.

In 1643, when Charles I fled from Gloucester after its abortive siege during the Civil Wars, he was rowed across the river by a Mr Jelf. For his loyalty he was rewarded with the rights of the ferry at this point for himself and his descendants. Ever since, the Jelfs have carried on their activities there, which have also included farming and salmon fishing. Here is Mr Edward J. Jelf working the ferry against the background of the Boat Inn (1940s). The Misses Jelf run the inn at the present time.

The oil tanker at the top left of the photograph was of the type used throughout the last war to save transport by road and rail as much as possible.

Mr E. Jelf preparing his salmon nets at his slipway at Ashleworth. 1940s.

Elvers have always been netted in the Severn, either for sale or to make a dish for one's table. This 1940s photograph shows how it was done.

Taking the catch home to the Boat Inn.

Maisemore, in 1913, was a village of thatched cottages by the Severn, only about two miles downstream from Ashleworth. It is a good place from which to see the Severn Bore.

Severn Bore at Lower Parting

The Severn Bore, a wall of water funnelled up the river at high tides from the Bristol Channel, is diverted at Lower Parting, one branch going to Gloucester and the other to all the villages so far mentioned, up to Tewkesbury. A 1915 photograph.

1931. Mr J.A. Chamberlayne moving cattle out of Maisemore Ham. The farm tumbrel was made by Morris and Ellis.

1920s. Mr Benjamin Etheridge was both postman and village carpenter.

1920s. The Forge at Maisemore, 150 years old. Mr Nelmes was the blacksmith from 1916 until his death in 1941. Horses were shod, iron tyres were put on the wheels of waggons and carts and agricultural implements were repaired.

1906. The Ship Inn, Maisemore. The wall, plastered with notices, was one way of drawing the attention of the locals to events which were pending. Notices tended to wear away with wind and rain until new ones were plastered over them.

1890. Maisemore School, teachers and pupils.

Tirley is another village whose history has been influenced by the Severn. It is readily approachable from Tewkesbury by way of the Haw Bridge. The motor car, motor bike and side-car are of 1924 vintage. Many of the houses seen here have since been demolished.

1908. Tirley church. It is built of blue lias and the tower is roughcast. It has features dating from the thirteenth to the nineteenth century.

Tirley church clock was built by John Carter, a wheel-wright, using pieces of discarded agricultural implements and other odds and ends, such as a chaff cutter, scythe, drill, separator, winnowing machine, farmyard weights and a cannon ball. It was installed in October 1918 as a memorial to Second Lieutenant George Edward Fowler, a Tirley farmer, killed near Ypres in 1917. John Carter cared for his clock, winding it every Wednesday and Saturday until his death in 1945, at the age of 80.

1920. Haw Bridge Inn, Tirley, with the Severn below. There has been an inn at Haw since 1662.

1920. This bridge, opened in 1825 was the first to be built at Haw. It superseded the Old Haw Passage or ferry.

In 1958 a barge-tanker hit the Haw bridge and completely demolished it.

Old cottage at Haw, 1870, since demolished under bridge and road-widening schemes.

Tirley School, 1921. It has been closed and converted into a house.

The first Haw bridge was subject to tolls and the toll-house on the east side is shown here. 1910. Tolls were abandoned after 1890.

Tirley school staff and children in 1894.

Town Street, Tirley.

1921. This is part of the older village which was by-passed when a new road was built under the Haw Bridge scheme.

Wigwood, Tirley

1930. Wigwood is typical of many farms in the area and is the home of the Hopkins family. Deceased members are commemorated on tablets and a brass plaque in the church, the first of which is dated 1789.

1930. The Severn was a means of transporting bales of hay and straw from local farms to the Midlands.

1940. Yew Tree Cottage, which once served as a shop for the people of Hasfield and outlying parts of Tirley, is now the home of Mr and Mrs A. Munn.

A corner of Tirley village, 1906.

1930. A popular way of traversing the narrow lanes of the Vale of Gloucester was by horse and trap. Mr A. Munn and his brother-in-law are all set to do so.

1930s. Some crew members of the barge *Dove*.

1928. This was a drought year, and these men of Staunton, a village on rising ground to the west of Tirley, are collecting water for livestock from a local stream which was still running clearly.

Staunton school, 1913.

1907. The cows are dual-purpose shorthorns, a popular breed at that time. The Swan Inn was, and still is, a popular house for villagers and visitors.

1928. South-west of Staunton, across the river Leadon, is Upleadon village. St Mary's church is unique in having a timber-framed tower dated c.1500.

At Redmarley, Glos (No. 1)

North of Upleadon, and making a triangle with Staunton, is Redmarley, 1910. Much of the village is Tudor.

Rose and Crown, Redmarley.

1917. This inn catered particularly for motorists and cyclists, though the Great War had, by now, considerably reduced its trade.

1912. Just over a mile from Tewkesbury, along the Gloucester Road, stands the old Odessa Inn. It was well patronised by cyclists' clubs in Edwardian days.

1904. Beside the Odessa, the road turns into the village of Tredington. The church is Norman, with a rebuilt timber-framed belfry of 1883. Embedded in the floor of the porch is a fossil ichthyosaurus, nine feet long.

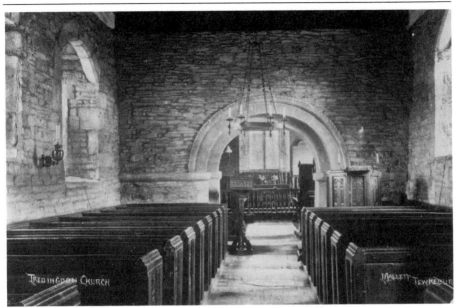

Tredington church interior, lit by candles and oil lamps. 1900.

1905. Tredington school, with Miss Clayton and Mrs Harris.

The Reverend Webster outside Manor Farm. He was village priest for 53 years. He died 8 November 1936.

The Castleton beagles passing Tredington church. The meet was at Manor Farm, 1958.

The Reverend Webster showing some friends the thatched barns of the village, a few years before his death.

Old Post Office, Tredington, pulled down 29 years ago.

Blacksmith's shop, Tredington. 1892. At the horse's head is William Bartlett, the blacksmith, and near the wheel of the cart is the Reverend Webster. The three children, Alice (in the pram), Eliza (pushing it), and Clara (in white pinafore) belonged to the Hawker family.

1927. Mr Bert Pitman is on the binder, and Arthur Hallings is riding the trace-horse. The tied sheaves were ejected when the three-pronged fork of the machine turned over and out.

Sidney Gilder on the rake which gathered up any loose straws of corn after the crop had been carried to the rickyard. The two-month-old colt refused to leave its mother and kept at her side all day long. 1940s, at Hardwick.

1879. Haymaking scene at Stonehouse Farm, Tredington.

1918. Typical farmyard scene, with threshing gang. Such outfits toured whole districts after harvest and throughout the winter.

1892. Tredington National School, 1890. The Revd and Mrs Webster are on the right. The teacher, on the left, is Mrs Belcher.

1898. Tredington school children and staff. The age range and dress are worthy of note.

1870. Historic stone house, Tredington. It was demolished this century and its windows sent to America. King Edward IV is reputed to have slept here the night before the Battle of Tewkesbury, in 1471.

Tredington cricket club fancy dress. 1929.

Chaceley Church stands to the west of the Severn, opposite Deerhurst on the east bank. It has a Norman chancel arch, and some thirteenth-century features, but a good deal of restoration occurred in 1882.

1890. Chaceley Hall. This beautiful building dates from 1470, with sixteenth-century additions on the north and south, all timber-framed on a high stone base. The farm raised beef and dairy cattle, arable crops and had very good orchard trees which originated from Long Ashton Research Station. Standing by the gate are Mr George Lane and his son, Henry Arthur Lane.

1939. Nearly every farm in the district had orchards from which cider was produced in large quantities. This is Mr W.H. Lane, whose grandfather and father are in the previous photograph, with his crop of apples.

1939. This is the mill-chase, turned by a horse, to produce apple pulp.

1939. Pressing the pulp between hessian mats to squeeze out the juice.

The cider was put into wooden barrels and allowed to mature for about a year. Mr Lane is sampling last year's cider. Cheers!

PHOTOGRAPH CREDITS

Mrs M. Apperley, Dr. R.B. Barnes, Mr F.B. Bigland, Miss B.L. Chamberlayne, Mrs G. Chandler, Mr C.H. Chatham, Mr W. Deacon, Revd J. Evans, Mrs A. Finnigan, Gloucestershire Records Office, Mrs M. Hedges, Mrs R. Hopkins, The Misses Jelf, Mr W.H. Lane, Mr & Mrs A. Munn, Miss F.E. Nelmes, Mrs N. Newman, Mrs A. Parker, Mr B.E. Pegler, Mrs J. Reynolds, Miss R. Stephens, Mr A. Sutton, Mrs G. Warner, Miss P. Warner, Mr & Mrs E. White, Mr & Mrs J. Yorke.

Thanks also to the many Parish Clerks and their Councillors for their help and interest.